HIT ME AGAIN!
(I Can Still Hear The Swine)

Also compiled by Jack Aspinwall:

KINDLY SIT DOWN!

HIT ME AGAIN!

(I Can Still Hear The Swine)

*More After-Dinner Stories
from the Houses of Parliament*

compiled by
JACK ASPINWALL, MP
Illustrated by Timothy Jaques

BUCHAN & ENRIGHT, PUBLISHERS
LONDON

First published in 1984 by
Buchan & Enright, Publishers, Limited
53 Fleet Street, London EC4Y 1BE

Copyright © Jack Aspinwall 1984

All rights reserved. No part of this publication may be
reproduced, stored in a retrieval system, or transmitted,
in any form or by any means, electronic, mechanical,
photocopying, recording, or otherwise, without the prior
permission in writing of the publishers.

British Library Cataloguing in Publication Data

Hit me again!
  1. English wit and humour
  I. Aspinwall, Jack
  828'.91407'08   PN6175

  ISBN 0-907675-31-X

*In the course of the production of this book there may have been a
number of changes of Members' positions in the Houses of
Parliament. While every effort has been made to keep up with all
these changes, it has, inevitably, not been possible to make all the
necessary alterations.*

Photoset in North Wales by
Derek Doyle & Associates, Mold, Clwyd
Printed in Great Britain by
Richard Clay (The Chaucer Press) Ltd,
Bungay, Suffolk

To

Brenda, my wife, who in 30 years of marriage has never lost her sense of humour.

Margaret Thatcher for her example and encouragement.

James Callaghan for kindly writing the Foreword.

Barbara and Madge for helping to make it all happen.

FOREWORD
by
the Right Honourable
James Callaghan, MP

Jack Aspinwall tells me that the publication of his first book of after dinner stories *Kindly Sit Down* resulted in the Airey Neave Memorial Trust benefiting to the extent of £5,000 from the proceeds, and as many as sixteen other charities also received donations.

A Member of Parliament's life is a busy one, and our grateful thanks are due to him for taking on an extra chore in compiling this second volume.

Thanks also to those of my Parliamentary colleagues who have provided the raw material. I thought I knew all the jokes that were ever told, but even so they have dug out some that were new to me.

Members of Parliament have no scruples about 'pinching' one another's stories, and I have no doubt that some of these will be told many times in the years ahead as garnish to our otherwise stodgy speeches.

Meantime, I hope that Jack Aspinwall's book will enjoy a large sale to hard-pressed after dinner speakers, and once more benefit his chosen charities.

James Callaghan

Keith Best, MP

A speaker at a dinner droned on at interminable length until one of the guests, seated at the end of the table, could take it no longer. He picked up an empty wine bottle, most of the contents of which he had consumed himself, and hurled it towards the speaker. Unfortunately, being somewhat inebriated, his aim was bad and rather than hitting the speaker the bottle struck the Chairman who was seated beside him. As he clutched his head and sank beneath the table the Chairman was heard to exclaim, 'Hit me again, I can still hear the swine.'

INTRODUCTION
by
Jack Aspinwall, MP

My second book of after-dinner stories and anecdotes has been so much fun to put together, and first of all I am very grateful to all those wonderful, busy people who have made a contribution and spared a little thought for others – the net proceeds of this volume will also go to a wide range of charities.

Hit Me Again! (I Can Still Hear the Swine), like my first book, *Kindly Sit Down!* will I hope prove to be a useful handbook for those involved in speech-making, and will spread a little humour and fun.

The idea occurred to me after my unsuccessful parachute jump for charity whilst lying in hospital recovering from a fractured spine – I never realised that I would end by compiling a best-selling book that would be sold around the world, nor that I would go on to compile another one. This new collection will, I am sure, give the reader a great deal of pleasure – a measure of the popularity of the first volume in the House of Commons Library is that the book is chained to the Librarian's desk – just out of reach of the photocopier!

These books can be used for raising funds for charity, and during the past year I have been able to give donations to many charities from the proceds of *Kindly Sit Down!*. Earlier in 1984 I arranged for RSM Ken Yeoman of the 'Red Devils' parachute team to present a donation of £5,000 from the proceeds of the book to Baroness Airey of Abingdon for the

Airey Neave Memorial Trust. Sergeant Major Yeoman saved one of his colleagues from certain death during a parachute jump by catching him in mid-air, but the way Ken fell meant that he is now paralysed. Ken, who was awarded the BEM for his action, trained the 'loony' intrepid Parliamentary parachute team, and they turned out in force on this occasion to pay tribute to their brave trainer.

You will enjoy this book – it contains the prized possessions of many Parliamentarians and others – their favourite after-dinner stories.

In an effort to promote improved overseas trade and jobs for one of my constituency businesses, a meeting was arranged between a trade attaché group from a foreign government and the chairman of a local company at the East India Club in London. I was standing just inside the impressive entrance waiting for my colleagues when I noticed Denis Thatcher there, whom I had met briefly on a couple of occasions. I went over and introduced myself as one of the Prime Minister's 'boys'. He was very pleasant and we chatted briefly until his friend arrived and he went into the dining-room for lunch. Eventually I settled down for a meal with my guests. Some time later Denis Thatcher came past my table, stopped, greeted us all, and said – 'Jack, how nice to see you again so soon.' He made my day!

Arriving in Rome by Air from the Far East in the early hours of the morning, I took a bus from the airport to the centre of Rome, then a taxi to my hotel. The taxi driver was extremely friendly and helpful. When I arrived at the hotel he took the luggage out of the boot of his car, and I paid him and gave him a tip. He immediately shook my hand, patted me on the back and kissed me on both cheeks! This EEC business is being taken too far, I thought. Deeply embarrassed I went into the hotel, walked up the stairs, and got to thinking. I then realized that I had given the taxi driver £25.00 instead of £2.50, and also a tip to boot!

Shortly after Winston Churchill left the Conservatives and joined the Liberals, he took a young lady out to dinner. She looked up at him coquettishly and remarked with some audacity, 'There are two things I don't like about you, Mr Churchill.' 'And what are they?' 'Your new politics, and your moustache.' 'My dear madam,' he replied suavely, 'pray do not disturb yourself – you are not likely to come in contact with either!'

It is said that Disraeli, when Prime Minister of England, was known particularly for his excellent memory. He was asked how he managed to remember all those names and never offend anyone by appearing not to recognise Members of Parliament on sight. The Prime Minister replied, 'When I meet a man whose name I cannot remember, I give myself two minutes: then if it is a hopeless case, I always say – "And how is the old complaint?" '

One of the guests at a fund-raising party in my new constituency of Wansdyke was a 94-year-old lady to whom I was introduced. She spoke softly and I didn't quite hear her name, and I asked her to repeat it. The remark she made certainly made me think, for she gently replied, 'When introductions take place the name you always hear is your own!'

Lord Carrington, CH, KCMG, MC, PC, JP, DL

A schoolboy was asked what he knew about Socrates.

He replied: 'Socrates was a Greek. He made speeches and was poisoned.'

David Heathcoat-Amory, FCA, MP

A Chinese cook was serving in a British regiment in the Second World War. He spoke very little English. One day he was badly wounded and was taken back to the field hospital.

He was put in intensive care and his bed was surrounded by life-support systems of every kind. Despite this it was obvious that he had not long to live, and the Padre was called.

The Padre approached the bed and bent over the Chinaman, who immediately took a turn for the worse and appeared to be very near death. When the Padre asked if there was any last wish or confession, the dying man frantically signalled for paper and pencil. This was quickly brought and the man scribbled some words in Chinese before he gave up the struggle and sank back dead.

The Padre was very moved by this. Clearly it contained some last message to be passed on to friends and loved ones. He reverently sent the piece of paper to be translated. When it was returned, the Padre opened it and read: 'Get your foot off the bloody oxygen pipe!'

Lord Shackleton, KG, OBE, PC

A Life Peer has a special novelty value – like a mule – no pride of ancestry and no hope of posterity.

Michael Lord, MP

While canvassing during the last General Election I came across a house with a bunch of flowers, recently delivered, on the doorstep. No one answered my knock and my energetic personal assistant, instead of popping my 'Sorry to have missed you' card through the letter box, laid it against the bunch of flowers.

The next morning a delightful note arrived for me at my campaign headquarters. It read: 'Mrs Roberts of 26, Willow Walk, is sorry she was out when you called, thank you for the lovely bunch of flowers, and will most certainly be voting Conservative.'

Neil Kinnock, PC, MP

I am repeatedly told that the greatest polar opposites can co-operate and in this business of politics it seems like useful advice. I treat the theory with some suspicion and not very long ago I was tackled by a personal manager of a major corporation, who said that he quite agreed with me on a lot of things but was exasperated by my aggressive view of the incompatibility of classes. And, after the argument had raged he said that he would prove to me how the most incompatible temperaments could get on with each other.

Whereupon he took me out to London Zoo and to a cage in which there was a great grey wolf with fangs dripping, accompanied in the cage by a sweet little spring lamb gambolling around in the corner. I was astounded, deeply impressed and I turned to him – this miracle worker – and said, 'How do you manage that?' And he told me: 'It's easy: we put a fresh lamb in twice a day.'

Malcolm Rifkind, MP

An Englishman, a Frenchman and a Russian were discussing the nationality of Adam and Eve.

The Englishman said, 'Here is a woman who gives her husband the apple, the only food she has. Only an English woman would behave in such a way.'

The Frenchman said, 'No, no, you are quite wrong. Here are a man and woman having lunch, naked in the garden. Only Frenchmen would behave in such a way.'

'No, no, comrades,' said the Russian, 'you don't know what you are talking about. Here are two people, they have no clothes to wear, hardly any food to eat and they think they are in paradise. They must be Russians.'

Sir Shuldham Redfern, KCVO, CMG

A story to demonstrate the power of the press:

There was a man in a train reading the *Daily Telegraph*. He read a page, tore it out, and threw it out of the window. He then tore out another page and threw it out of the window, and continued to do so until the man opposite, who had been watching in amazement, said: 'Why do you do that?'

'To keep away the elephants,' was the reply.

'But there are no elephants here.'

'You see,' said the *Telegraph* reader, tearing out yet another page and casting it out of the train window, 'it works!'

Lord Airedale

A trainer of guide-dogs for the blind remarked that people expect too much of a guide-dog, and told of a blind girl arriving with her dog in Cardiff for the first time.

She asked a lady passer-by the way to her destination. The lady bent down and said to the dog, 'You go to the third set of traffic lights, turn left and it's the second turning on the right.'

Jonathan Sayeed, MP

The directors of two leading distillers of Scotch whisky attended a funeral together. Despite being rivals in the whisky trade, for the sake of appearances, they were prepared to share a drink before the service. When one asked the other what he would have, he said he would like a whisky of his own brand; to his surprise, when buying the drinks his rival ordered the same drink for himself. To explain this seeming lack of 'patriotism', his host explained, as he passed him his glass, that he had thought it would be unseemly for them to attend a funeral with the smell of whisky on their breath.

Jeremy Hanley, MP

A lot of people believe that it must be easy being a Member

of Parliament, but it reminds me of the story of Mr Tommy Trinder who was in his Rolls-Royce in the Fulham Road when he stalled at traffic lights. He tried his best to get the car started, getting more and more flustered, but not nearly as irritated as the taxi driver who was pulled up behind him. The taxi driver started peeping his horn and got more and more animated with impatience. After about five minutes Mr Trinder got out of his car, walked back to the taxi behind him and invited the driver to wind the window down. When the driver had done so Tommy Trinder put his hand through the taxi window and banged his hand repeatedly on the horn. 'I'll tell you what,' he said, 'let's swop. I'll do this and you start the bloody car!'

Lord Ingrow, OBE, TD, JP, DL

A famous politician found only one person present at a farmers' meeting he was due to address. Wondering whether to proceed, he asked his audience, who said, 'If I only had one hen I would feed it.'

The politician thereupon delivered a complete and masterly speech, and enquired if the farmer had enjoyed it. 'Aye,' said the farmer, 'but if I'd only one hen I wouldn't have given it a bucketful.'

Ken Hargreaves, MP

Despite an excellent and varied menu in the House of Commons dining room, a Boycott curry has not yet appeared on it.

A Boycott curry is exactly the same as any other curry, but the runs take longer to come.

Lord Mancroft, KBE, TD

Early in June 1944 I happened, together with several others, to find myself on the beaches in Normandy. One afternoon, I received a message from my CO to the effect that the Corps Commander was coming along our part of the beach, to see what we were up to, and would I please straighten myself up and go and welcome the great man.

Well, it so happened that we weren't up to very much that particular afternoon. There seemed to be a lull in the proceedings and we were taking advantage of this lull to carry out a little house-keeping – humping ammunition, digging gun-pits, washing our socks, writing home to mother and taking the fuses out of those horrible Teller-mines.

In due course I ran the Corps Commander to earth. He was watching a working party under the command of our Bombardier Bean, who was leaning on a shovel, watching the Corps Commander – no saluting, or anything like that – all very *Daily Mirror* and democratic.

I was a mite embarrassed by all this nonchalance so, in a breathy stage-whisper, I said, 'What's the matter, Bombardier? Have you never seen a Lieutenant-General before?'

'Oh yes, sir,' he said, 'of course I have. But that's the first one I've ever seen standing on a live Teller-mine.'

John Corrie, MP

Canvassing as a new Member in 1964 I was in a Labour area when a very attractive young lady answered the door.

I explained who I was and she invited me in to tell her about Conservative policies. Thinking I had a 'doubtful'

and might be able to persuade her to support me, I went in and gave my long story on our policies. At this point I was offered a cup of tea which I took. I was then shown round the council house to see the problems of dampness which I might be able to help with.

Two and a half hours later after more questions and answers, I edged towards the door, content that I'd won a vote in a strong Labour area, when the lady in question said in her best Scottish accent, 'I'd better just tell you, son, that my husband is the Chairman of the local Labour party and I'm the secretary, and that's two and a half hours less canvassing you'll do this afternoon!''

Baroness Airey of Abingdon

Winston Churchill had a meeting with President Roosevelt who urgently wanted to consult him about some important matter. The President knocked on his door and entered but was rather disconcerted to see the rotund and pink form of the Prime Minister in his bath, and started hurriedly to back out in his wheelchair. Churchill said robustly: 'Come in, Mr President. England has nothing to hide from her allies.'

Roger Gale, MP

A chief executive gave an aspiring young politician a dog as a present. Their ways parted but some years later crossed again.

'How's the dog?' enquired the chief executive.

'Very depressing,' said the politician. 'When I became a councillor it would walk to heel. Then I became a committee chairman and he learned to offer his paw and shake hands. While I was Leader of the Council he would lie on his back with his paws in the air, but now that I am Mayor all he will do is sit and eat and bark!'

Lord Grade

When I was going to produce *Jesus of Nazareth* I was asked by one of the press if I could name the Twelve Apostles. I said, 'Mark, Luke, Peter and Paul', and then said, 'I can't tell you the rest of the names as I haven't finished reading the script.'

Cyril Smith, MBE, MP

Bloke in top bunk shouts out, 'Look out, I'm going to be sick.'

Bloke in bottom bunk did – and he was!

Neil Thorne, OBE, TD, MP

On the death of a lady living in a block of flats, the undertakers were called in to remove her body. On the way down the stairs, the man in front slipped, the coffin crashed to the floor, whereupon the lady sat up. Three years later she 'died' again, and when the men came to collect the body this time the husband cautioned them, asking them to avoid another terrible accident.

The Viscount St Davids

There had been a by-election in one of the great deserted

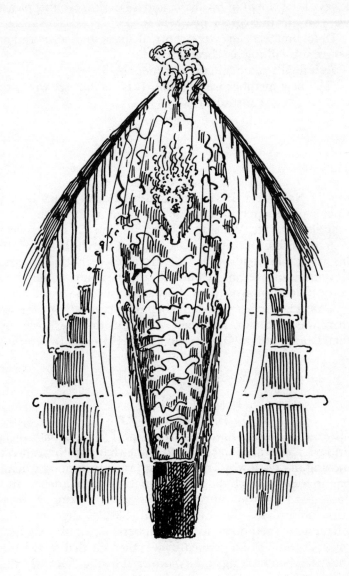

areas of the North of Scotland, and a London evening paper was commenting on the new MP.

Unfortunately they were short of space and some rather severe sub-editing had been needed.

As it finally came out, the comment read:

'The new member wears a kilt. It takes him six weeks to cover his huge constituency!'

Susan Ketelsen

On 29 November 1974, the Stretford Constituency held a Centenary Dinner to honour the memory of their MP's grandfather, Sir Winston Churchill. The Chairman was charged with proposing a toast to 'The Churchill Family'. In his speech he made much of the roles of both Baroness Churchill and Minnie Churchill and how much they had contributed towards their husbands' success; with great emphasis he further stated that behind every really great man there was a woman. The guest of honour that night was the then Leader of HM Opposition, the Rt Hon E.G.R. Heath.

Tim Sainsbury, MP

On one occasion, I was asked to speak in a debate on a Friday. The debate was delayed somewhat and things were moving rather slowly. The time was fast approaching when I had to leave to catch the train down to my constituency, so I apologised to the other speakers after making a brief contribution to the debate and hastily departed the Chamber. I sped down to the Members' Entrance to collect my coat, only to be greeted by a rather startled look from the Attendant looking at the monitor showing that I was still speaking. As I ran out of the door, a Labour Member was heard to shout, 'Don't let him out until he has finished speaking!'

Richard Hickmet, MP

I was a guest of the Turkish/Cyprus Government in August 1983 and visited that country with my wife and daughter who, at the time, was two and a half years old. We were invited to attend a lunch with the President, the Prime Minister and the rest of the Cabinet. In typical hospitable fashion our hosts insisted that we should bring our daughter as well, as the Turks love children.

We told her repeatedly that she would have to behave herself because she would be meeting the President and the Prime Minister.

The lunch went extremely well with our daughter, Sophie, crawling all over President Denktash and repeatedly asking him if he really was the President. His good humour increased on each occasion that he answered, 'Yes, I am indeed the President.'

She then turned her attentions to the Prime Minister and asked him, 'Are you the Prime Minister? Are you really the Prime Minister?' in a very sceptical voice. He too beamed and said that indeed he was. Whereupon she said, 'Oh, no, you're not. Margaret Thatcher is the Prime Minister.'

Joe Ashton, MP

When tempers were running very high during the Six Days' War between the Arabs and the Israelis there was an extremely partisan atmosphere in the House. Christopher Mayhew, the then Labour MP for Greenwich was really angry, excited and sounding off on the back benches about what the Israelis had done to the Arabs.

'The Arabs never said they would drive the Jews into the sea,' he protested. 'I will give £5,000 to anyone who can ever prove that such a statement was ever made.'

He paused for dramatic effect and a small Jewish voice cried, 'If I hear six perhaps we could do business.'

A. Cecil Walker, JP, MP

Mrs Appleby had had a tiff with her maid and fired her. The maid was packed and ready to leave, and took the opportunity to get a few things off her mind.

'It might surprise you to know that your husband thinks I'm a better cook and housekeeper than you are. He told me so himself.'

Mrs Appleby made no comment.

'And another thing, I'm better in bed than you are, too.'

'I suppose my husband told you that as well,' snapped Mrs Appleby.

'No,' said the maid, 'the chauffeur did.'

Lord Wolfenden, CBE

I had just come back from an Old Boys' Dinner at a school where I was once Headmaster. The after-dinner hours were filled by an endless stream of men, fat, bald, puce-faced, who approached me one by one with the inevitable words 'You don't remember me, sir.'

I was irresistibly reminded of a predecessor of mine who was known to be absent-minded, and deliberately played on it. When an Old Boy – any Old Boy – re-visited his school and challenged the Headmaster's memory in the traditional

27

way, the deliberately absent-minded old man interrupted –
'Stop! I know your name perfectly well but I *cannot*
remember your face.' He got away with that for twenty
years.

David Harris, MP

Modesty is not a characteristic normally associated with
politicians. But long before credit cards became a necessity
of life, Clem Attlee, the then Labour Prime Minister, was
having a quiet lunch in Soho of all places, with an up-and-
coming politician, the Earl of Longford. At the end of the
meal, both men found they had insufficient cash on them to
pay the bill. Longford suggested that the Prime Minister
could always pay by cheque but Attlee countered by saying,
'The trouble is I'm not known here.'

Greg Knight, MP

Members of Parliament get all sorts of problems at their
regular constituency surgeries. One young man who was in
doubt over his matrimonial intentions went to see his MP.
He unfolded his heart to his local Member and explained
that he was not sure what he should do. He needed advice
on whether he should marry a wealthy but ugly old widow
who appeared to be chasing after him or whether he should
marry the pretty – but penniless – young girl that he loved.
The MP had no hesitation in giving his advice.

MP: 'Listen to your heart, son, and take the advice it gives
you. Marry the girl you love.'

Young man: 'Yes, I am grateful. On reflection, I know that
you are right. Thank you very much. How can I ever
repay you?'

MP: 'Give me the old crow's address.'

28

The Earl de la Warr, DL

'No, no, a hundred times no,' said the centipede, crossing her legs.

Admiral of the Fleet Lord Hill-Norton, GCB

Before the war, when there were several hundred destroyers in the Fleet (more's the pity that there aren't today); they habitually berthed in harbour in pairs between two buoys – and a splendid sight it was to see 50 or so of them in Sliema Creek in Malta.

Hands were usually called at 0600 in those days and turned to at 0630 for an hour's work before breakfast, getting their ship bright and shiny to start the day. One summer's morning in 1935 the First Lieutenant of one V and W Class destroyer came on deck a bit early and noticed at once that his 'chummy ship' was very low in the water. It appeared that an inlet valve had failed and the resultant flooding through the night had put HMS *Nonsuch* down a good three feet in the water. He at once sent a message to his 'oppo' next door.

The early bird was still watching when the first sleepy sailors appeared on deck next door, and he had the pleasure of hearing one of them, spotting the disaster, bawl out to his mates, 'Crikey, some bugger's pinched our effing water-line.'

Nicholas R. Winterton, MP

A story told to me some years ago relates to a couple who, after a number of years of marraige, were having a typical domestic row when the husband suddenly left the room and went up to the bedroom where he began to pack. His wife, somewhat surprised, enquired as to where he intended to go and how he intended to live. He replied, in a very positive and offhand way, that he intended to go to an island he knew, where they paid 50p every time you made love. The wife casually requested further information, wanting to know how her husband expected to live on £4.50 a year.

Greg Knight, MP

One evening a policeman strolling down a dimly lit street noticed a large expensive-looking car with a House of Commons badge on the windscreen. Inside the car, the officer could see a man in the driving seat and a girl sitting alone in the back. Somewhat curious, he approached and noticed that the driver was reading a book and the young girl was sitting in the back of the car knitting. The officer opened the driver's door and asked the man what he was doing.

'Well, surely, officer, it is obvious. I am reading a book,' he intoned.

The officer was completely perplexed. 'Well, sir, what is your occupation and how old are you?' he enquired.

'I am a Member of Parliament and, if it has any relevance to the situation, I am forty-one years of age,' the MP answered.

The policeman, still none the wiser, opened the rear door

of the car and addressed the young girl, 'Well, what are you doing, miss?' he asked.

'Well, surely, you can see, officer, that I am knitting,' the pretty young thing replied.

'And how old are you, miss?' he asked.

'Well, officer, in ten minutes I will be sixteen.'

The Earl of Elgin and Kincardine, KT, JP, DL

During a visit to Cape Town some twenty years ago, my host was a Scottish bank manager. I asked him how long he had been abroad.

'Sixty years,' was his reply.

'Were you ever homesick?' I asked.

'Never,' said he, 'for you must understand I get home every other year to see my wife.'

Ivan Lawrence, QC, MP

The Lord Chancellor, Lord Hailsham (formerly Quintin Hogg) told a story at a legal dinner about a felon called Hogg who appeared before Lord Chancellor Bacon early in the seventeenth century. Hogg was found guilty and asked if there was any reason why sentence should not be passed upon him in accordance with the law. He replied, 'Yes, for I claim kinship with your Lordship.'

'How so?' demanded the great judge.

'Because,' said the felon. 'Hogg is verily akin to Bacon.'

'Quite so,' responded the Lord Chancellor, 'but only when the hog hath been well and truly hanged.'

Reg Prentice, PC, MP

A large industrial firm wanted to employ an economic adviser. They put an advertisement into the papers setting out the requirements and offering a good salary. They also specified that the successful applicant must only have one arm.

Several economists applied. They were puzzled about the one-arm requirement, but thought it must be a mistake. They were all turned down.

One of them asked: 'I have all the other requirements. Why turn me down because I have two arms?' The managing director explained that he was sick and tired of listening to advisers who said, 'On the one hand this, on the other hand that.'

Joe Ashton, MP

It is a very tense debate in the House of Commons and Willie Hamilton is accusing Harold Wilson of ratting on his commitment to the Common Market.

'First he is for the Market,' thundered Willie, 'then he is against. What does he stand for? Is he in or out? This is not the politics of leadership – it is the politics of coitus interruptus!'

There was a shocked silence, then an indignant voice called, 'Withdraw!'

Nicholas R. Winterton, MP

Cheshire has always been blessed with excellent Chief Constables, and most of them have possessed considerable skill in carrying out their difficult task, as well as a sense of humour. One such Chief Constable was presented with a set of plans for a new Police Headquarters, and asked to comment. After a lengthy study of what was a fairly complicated set of drawings, he only made one request of the architect, and that was that the urinals in the gentlemen's lavatories should be raised some six inches. When asked to justify this strange request, he merely replied that he had always sought to keep his men on their toes.

Lord Redesdale

Two tick-tack men went to the funeral of a friend in a Catholic church. As they had never been to church before they were rather nervous and sat at the back. Their consternation was complete when the priest came in and crossed himself; one tick-tack man turned to the other and said, 'I don't like the look of that, poor old Charlie's starting at 100/1!'

Robert Atkins, MP

On the day after the Election, a defeated candidate was seen walking down the street with a big grin on his face. When asked why, he said, 'If you'd seen the election promises I made, you'd be glad I lost!'

William F. Newton Dunn, MEP

The late Henry Ford I was visiting Dublin and arranged to make a donation of $5,000 towards a new local hospital. But next morning the Mayor called to apologise: 'I am sorry, sir, but the newspapers have printed that it was $50,000 and it will look very bad to have to print a correction.' Henry Ford replied by handing over a cheque for the balance, but said there would be one condition: 'There must be a plaque on the hospital wall with these words, "I was a stranger and ye took me in".'

John Mulkern, Managing Director, British Airports Authority

An Admiral and a Bishop, who loathed each other, were both in full regalia waiting for a flight from an airport during a snowstorm. The Bishop couldn't resist it: 'How long will this flight be delayed, steward', he said to the Admiral. 'Madam, if I were in your condition I wouldn't travel', came the snappy reply.

Michael Blond

Having given a particularly long and, for his audience, narcoleptic speech the night before, a pompous businessman berated his PA:

'What the hell do you think you're playing at, Smith,' he fumed. 'I asked you to write me a twenty-minute speech and the bloody thing went on for a whole hour!'

'But I *did* only write you a twenty-minute speech, sir,' said the puzzled PA. Then, after a moment's thought: '*And* I attached two carbon copies.'

Lord Hughes, CBE, PC, DL

Three prisoners, newly arrived at a Soviet prison camp, were talking. Prisoner number one said he had been sentenced to ten years. He could not rise in the morning and was persistently late for work; he was imprisoned for sabotaging the state's industrial effort. Prisoner number two said he also had been given ten years, but in his case he always arrived at work earlier than he had to; he was sentenced for spying for the West. When the third one was asked how long he was to be there and why, he replied that he also was in for ten years, but he was never late and never early at work. Why therefore was he there, he was asked. He replied, 'They discovered I had a Swiss watch.'

Roger Gale, MP

A Russian peasant applied to join the Communist Party. 'Are you prepared to sacrifice your house for the sake of the Party?' he was asked.

'Yes,' he replied.

'Are you prepared to sacrifice your car for the sake of the Party?' he was asked.

'Yes,' he replied.

'Are you prepared to sacrifice your wife for the sake of the Party?' he was asked.

'Yes,' he replied.

'Are you prepared to sacrifice your horse for the sake of the Party?' he was asked.

'No,' he said firmly.
'Why not?'
'Because I have a horse.'

Field-Marshal Lord Harding of Petherton, GCB, CBE, DSO
For those like Lord mayors who often have to make more than one speech on the same day:

'I am envious of the parson who said he could get away with the same sermon at morning and evening service by taking his teeth out in the morning.'

Nicholas Lyell, QC, MP
Recently, when visiting an ante-natal clinic used by my constituents, I saw on the wall a notice to young mothers about the benefits of vaccinations and other post-natal care. Above was the caption: 'Remember, the first year of life is the most dangerous.' Beneath this, someone had scrawled – 'The last is not without its hazards!'

Sir Kenneth Lewis, DL, MP
Three young drunks were apprehended by the police. They conferred together and decided to give false names, made up from names they could see when looking down the High Street.

The policeman asked the first one: 'What is your name?'

'Mark Spencer,' he said.

The second when asked said, 'Philip Sainsbury.'

The third, rather less bright, said, 'Ken Tucky Fried Chicken.'

Lord Hill of Luton, PC

Husband setting off for Masonic gathering – tarted up in glad rags. Wife, sitting quietly at home – contemplating a tired Welsh rabbit. She asks him:

'George, what would you do if you came home and found me in the arms of another man?'

His reply was instant: 'Shoot his guide-dog.'

A. Cecil Walker, JP, MP

When the Creator was making the world, he called Man aside and let him know that he was giving him twenty years of normal sex life. Man was very unhappy about this and asked the Creator for more – they were refused.

The monkey was then called, and offered twenty years. 'But I don't need twenty years,' protested the monkey. 'Ten will do.'

'May I have the extra ten years then?' pleaded Man and this time the Creator graciously agreed.

Then He called the noble lion and offered him twenty years. The lion didn't want more than ten either, so Man asked for the surplus and was granted ten more years.

Then came the donkey; he was also offered twenty years, but, as with the others, he said that ten years was ample. Man again begged for the spare ten years and got them.

This perhaps explains why man has twenty years of normal sex life, ten years of monkeying around, ten years lion about it and ten years of making an ass of himself.

Lord Grimthorpe, OBE, DL

Scene – Elderly American couple considering marriage.

Lady: 'Elmer, we have discussed everything, but what about *sex*?'

Elmer: 'My dear – infrequently, infrequently.'

Lady: 'Thank you, Elmer, but will you tell me if that is one word or two!'

The Marquess of Hertford, DL

A nonentity was boring the actress Coral Browne with a glowing description of the beauty of a much younger actress and ended up by saying 'You should have seen her when she was seventeen; her hair literally came down to her knees.'

Coral Browne smiled very sweetly and asked, 'Growing from where?'

Susan Ketelsen

In the wake of a much-publicised visit to the Stretford Constituency by the Rt Hon. Member for Down South, our MP was engaged in a walk-about in Old Trafford. A buxom West Indian lady accepted his handshake.

'And where do you live?' he enquired.

'Powell Street,' she answered.

'Oh, dear; unfortunate name, isn't it?'

'Yes, it is, but de worse ting is, me husband him called Enoch.'

40

The Viscount Caldecote, DSC

During the 1930s my father, then Sir Thomas Inskip, was Attorney-General, the chief law officer of the Government. One day he received the draft of a speech, to be made by His Majesty King George V, from the King's Private Secretary, with a request that he should look through it and make any comments he wished.

On reading it, my father could find nothing remotely controversial or inappropriate, and returned the speech saying he had no comments to make. But he was naturally mystified about why it had ever been sent to him.

Some time later he discovered that the King had scribbled in the margin of one paragraph a note, 'Refer to A.G.' The Secretary had assumed that 'A.G.' meant 'Attorney-General' – whereas in reality the note was to remind His Majesty, when delivering the speech, to refer to Almighty God at this point!

The Bishop of Chelmsford

The Vicar had just announced from the pulpit his forthcoming resignation. On leaving the church after the service he observed the old verger sobbing his heart out. He hastened to comfort him and said, 'You must not upset yourself, I don't doubt they will find you a new vicar as good as I am or better.'

To which the verger replied, 'I know, sir, that is what the last man said when he left, and it weren't true.'

Neil Thorne, OBE, TD, MP

Two Irishmen were engaged by British Telecom to put in telegraph poles. The foreman indicated a pile of about twenty poles at the end of one road, and showed them the marks where they were to be inserted. At the end of the day they went to collect their money and were asked by the foreman, who had been called away on other duties, how many they had planted. To his astonishment they told him three. The foreman pointed out rather curtly that his other team had planted fifteen. 'Ah,' said the first Paddy, 'but you should see how much of theirs is sticking out of the ground.'

Roger Gale, MP

A young and teetotal curate was due to give his first sermon. On the way to the church on Sunday morning he called in at the vicarage for a few words of encouragement from the boss. The vicar sat him down and, despite the young man's protests, poured him first one large glass of sherry and then a second, insisting that under the circumstances a little Dutch courage would be no bad thing.

After the service, and having delivered his maiden sermon, the young man returned to the vicarage for a de-briefing: 'Well, how did it go?' he asked.

'Not bad ... not bad at all,' said the vicar, 'but there were one or two minor errors. It was, you will now recall, the Israelites that beat the Philistines. It was not Goliath who slew David but David that slew Goliath. Oh ... and there's just one other thing. He did it with a pebble – not "a bloody great rock"!'

Lord Dean of Beswick

Commenting on the harpist in the Harcourt Room Restaurant in the House of Commons, First Peer said, 'We could do with this in the Lords.' Second Peer replied, 'Most of us have got one already, we are only waiting for the wings.'

Greg Knight, MP

Most of us, at some time or another, get accused of never admitting to our mistakes, but the biscuit is surely taken by one particular MP, who seeing someone across a crowded room, hurried over and said, 'Well, well, well, you have changed, Bill. You've lost a lot of weight, and your hair has gone all grey. I see you don't wear glasses any more and you've shaved off your beard. Crickey, Bill Jones – what on earth has happened to you?'

The man replied, 'But my name isn't Bill Jones, I'm Frederick Conway-Lyons.'

'Remarkable,' replied the MP. 'You've even changed your name.'

Lord Ironside

We solemnly go through all the business of introductions at conferences and parties nowadays and I often wonder what's in a name and why we do it, but it does cause amusement on many occasions. My name always seems to arouse interest abroad and I have always found that people cannot really understand how our parliamentary system works. Perhaps it's not surprising, when one looks at how the two Houses are constituted, that throughout my life I've always been labelled as one of Cromwell's Ironsides.

In America it conjures up an image of the USS *Constitution*, the first ironclad which was nicknamed 'Old Ironsides', so with my technology interests I have now learnt to introduce myself over there as 'New Ironsides'.

In Holland, a few years ago now, I found I was very popular suddenly and I couldn't understand why until I had to give my name at the Airport Duty Free Shop. The man behind the counter said, 'That's a very famous name. I've read about it in history.' Naturally I felt a hint of pride; the same thing happened a week later when a bright young girl said, 'That's a famous name.'

Being prepared for this, I said, 'You have seen it in the history books, I expect.'

'Oh no,' she said, 'I see him once a week on television!'

Rather deflated, I took comfort in consoling myself that the series could have been called 'A Man Called French'. After all, what's in a name?

Neil Hamilton, MP

Two Russians living in England were a bit homesick; but, because they had heard that things were a bit dodgy back in Russia, they decided that only one of them should return home and then write back about it. Before he left, the one going to Russia said, 'In case my letter is censored I'll write in black ink if things are all right and in red if they are not.'

Eventually the other chap got his letter. It was written in black ink and said, 'I am having a marvellous time in Russia. Life is wonderful and there is plenty of everything. The only thing you can't buy is red ink.'

The late Viscount Boyd of Merton, CH, DL

I once had a letter from an MP who had stumbled on the truth concerning a matter when it was not in the public's interest for me to tell him that his surmise was correct. I asked the Permanent Secretary at the Colonial Office how best it was for me to reply. He came up with –

Dear John,
I regret to inform you that your letter is not among those selected for a reply.

Tim Smith, MP

When he was Foreign Secretary in Ted Heath's Government, Sir Alex Douglas-Home (as he then was) visited Chairman Mao in Peking. He said to Mao: 'Mao, you and I are both great statesmen with a wealth of international experience. Sometimes I look back and I wonder how things might have turned out had chance played a different hand. For example,' he said, 'I wonder what would have happened if it had been Kruschev who had been assassinated and not Kennedy.'

Mao listened and thought for some time as he was wont to do. Then he said, 'Well, I don't think that Aristotle Onassis would have married Mrs Kruschev.'

Field-Marshal Lord Harding of Pertherton, GCB, CBE, DSO, MC

At one time in the Second World War carrier-pigeons were

introduced for use by forward troops to report progress in an offensive when, as happened more often than not, all telephone wires were cut by shellfire. There were no walkie-talkies or the like in those days. On one occasion everyone at a certain Divisional Headquarters engaged in an attack waited anxiously for the first pigeon to arrive. When it did the general and his senior staff officers rushed to the pigeon loft. The pigeon handler carefully removed the message and handed it at once to the general, whose face was white with dismay as he handed it to his senior staff officer, who read: 'I'm fed up with carrying this b——y bird.'

Cranley Onslow, MP

The O & M (Organisation & Methods) expert's report on Schubert's *Unfinished Symphony*:

1   The four oboe players were idle for long periods: work should be spread evenly over the whole orchestra to eliminate unprofitable peaks and troughs of activity.
2   All twelve violins appeared to be playing exactly the same tune: this represents excessive duplication. If a loud noise is really desired, it would be more economic to employ two violins and an amplifier.
3   Too much attention is given to the playing of demi-semi-quavers. All notes should be rounded up to the nearest semi-quaver. This would open the way for cost-saving through the employment of semi-skilled personnel or trainees.
4   There does not seem to be any obvious purpose in the repetition by the woodwind of a tune that has just been played by the strings. The elimination of this and other wasteful practices would reduce the length of the work by at least 15 minutes, and should have enabled the composer to finish the symphony without difficulty.

Lord King of Wartnaby

A very well known and very rich businessman was asked to address a class of students who were close to their degree graduation.

In describing his rise to fame and fortune he told them his story of how one day, when walking the streets as a penniless youngster, he became desperate to go to the lavatory.

It was a little time before he persuaded a passer-by to give him a penny.

He rushed down the steps of the public lavatory and to his great relief found a door open.

Having dealt with his problem he came back and went off and used his coin to buy some apples. He polished them up, wrapped them in tissue paper and sold them individually. He then bought some more and so on from street, to barrow, to shop, to a chain, to property and so on to his present situation.

At this point one of the students said, 'I'm sure you would like to find the man who gave you the penny.'

The speaker replied, 'I don't know about that, but I sure would like to meet the man who left the door open.'

Sir Anthony Meyer, Bt, MP

On his first parachute jump, Mick was told to jump clear of the aeroplane, count ten, and pull the rip-cord. He jumped, counted ten, and pulled. Nothing happened. As he hurtled towards the ground he saw a chap coming up equally fast towards him, with a large spanner in his hand. 'Excuse me,' he called out, 'Do you know anything about parachutes?'

'I'm afraid not,' came the answer. 'I don't know much about gas cookers, either.'

Sir Kenneth Lewis, DL, MP

Asked what the Minister's speech had been like, the new back-bencher, with engaging frankness, said: 'A bit like an ox's head; two good points and a lot of bull in between.'

Lord Cayzer

Some time ago I was reading a book entitled *The Later Cecils*, and I was struck by a legendary story which concerned Lord William Cecil, a one-time Bishop of Exeter and a man whose absent-mindedness was proverbial. On one occasion he failed to find his rail ticket when asked for it by an inspector.

'Don't trouble, my Lord,' the official assured him. 'We all know who you are.'

The Bishop replied, 'That is all very well, but without a ticket how do I know where I am supposed to be going?'

Nicholas Comfort, Daily Telegraph Political Staff

This story concerns a young farm labourer in an isolated village on the edge of the North Derbyshire coalfield, who on the outbreak of the last war was promptly conscripted down the pit. He was a strapping young lad and did well at the coal face, but from the very beginning he could not understand why he should, at the start of each shift, have to walk what seemed like miles from the bottom of the pit shaft to where he had left his pick, and the same distance back when he finished.

51

His second day at work, he asked the man next to him: 'Why do we have to walk miles and miles to reach the coal, and miles and miles back to the cage at night?'

'I wouldn't know about that,' said his mate. 'You'd best ask the overman.'

The next day he asked the overman the same question: 'Why do we have to walk miles and miles to reach the face, and miles and miles back to the cage at night?'

'I can't tell you that, lad,' said the overman. 'You'll have to ask the assistant manager.'

On the fourth day he met the assistant manager in the pit yard and put the question to him, his sense of waste all the greater because day by day the face was moving further away from the pit bottom.

The assistant manager could only nod sadly and say to him: 'I can't tell you that, lad. You'll have to ask the manager himself.'

The very next day, he came up from the pit bottom, having walked a few yards further even than on the fourth, to see the pit manager emerging from his ofice.

The young man walked straight up to him and asked: 'Why do we have to walk miles and miles to reach the coal face, and miles and miles back to the pit bottom at night?'

Taken aback, the manager turned to him and said: 'You can't ask questions like that. Don't you know there's a war on?'

'Oh, aye,' said the lad, whose knowledge of current affairs was limited. 'Who are we fighting?'

'Why, the Germans, of course,' said the manager.

'I'm not surprised,' replied the lad. 'We're pinching all their bloody coal.'

Lord Baker, OBE, FRS
Noah stood at the head of the gangway, running down from

the Ark, as the animals filed out, two by two. 'Go forth and multiply,' he chanted. Two snakes passed and said, rather stuffily, 'We can't, we're adders.'

A few weeks later Noah was strolling in the forest when he came to a clearing where a number of trees had been felled. To his delight he saw the snakes, surrounded by a family of little ones. 'What's this?' said he, 'I thought you couldn't multiply?' 'Well, we can't,' said the snakes, 'but we managed all right when we came across these logs.'

Nicholas R. Winterton, MP

There are many stories about the sparkling wit of that great politician and statesmen, Sir Winston Churchill. One relates to a brief meeting which he had, when he was Prime Minister, with his counterpart in the Republic of Ireland. Both countries were facing serious problems, and Churchill recalled that when he commented that, in his view, the situation in the United Kingdom was serious but not hopeless, the Irish Prime Minister replied that the situation in his country was hopeless but not serious.

Michael Stern, MP

At a very much earlier stage in my political career, I applied for selection at numerous parliamentary seats, up and down the country, most of them being held by the Labour Party with substantial majorities. Much to my surprise, my first interview was at a town in Yorkshire which was generally reckoned to be highly marginal, and, in accordance with normal practice, the Chairman of the Selection Committee wrote to me to tell me that I was required to attend for an interview of approximately half an hour but that I would not be required to make a speech, merely to answer questions.

I arrived at the constituency offices a little early, accompanied by my then girl-friend (now my wife) and shortly after we had both started work on the obligatory cups of weak tea, the previous interviewee came downstairs into the office and announced to all and sundry that he had to hurry away to get into his cricket whites. My wife claims that it was at this point she realised I had no chance whatsoever, since I could not claim to participate in Yorkshire's religion!

The Chairman invited me upstairs and as he was walking me across to a lone chair in a room which appeared otherwise packed, he invited me to make a ten-minute speech on why I thought I would be the ideal candidate for ——. Having no previous interview experience and having taken on trust his earlier letter, I do not think that I made a tremendous success of the speech although I did manage to keep going for most of the requisite ten minutes. He then called for questions and the first one was, 'Mr Stern, what can you, a foreigner from south of Doncaster, possibly have to say to the people of ——?'

Mentally at war between nerves and temper I managed to stammer out a reply, something to the effect that the problems of —— were the problems of the nation and that I was sure the electorate would find my southern accent quaint.

It was on the next question that I began to realise, like my wife before me, that the interviewing committee might not have been very interested because the second question was, 'Mr Stern, why aren't you married?' Still retaining my temper, I replied that the life of a prospective candidate could be somewhat upsetting to a family but that I did have a steady girl-friend, who I was sure would be of tremendous help in my campaign, and who had been educated in Yorkshire. The immediate supplementary question was, 'How long will she be steady?' At this point, I threw all caution to the winds and suggested that he invite her up and ask her the question himself but that I would not be responsible for the consequences. I cannot recollect any more of the interview.

The ferocity of this particular Selection Committee is perhaps evidenced by the fact that, by the time of the general election, they were on their third candidate, having already accepted and rejected two.

Neil Thorne, MP

The three biggest lies:
– Of course I'll love you as much in the morning.
– The cheque is in the post
– I'm from the Government and I am here to help you.

The three most difficult things to do:
– Write a witty after-dinner speech
– Climb a wall leaning towards you
– Kiss a woman leaning away from you.

Lord Croft

An elderly and rather absent-minded baronet was invited out to dinner. On taking leave of his host and hostess he remarked politely, 'It was very pleasant meeting you both again but I am afraid it must have been one of cook's off days and I must apologise for that.'

Jonathan Sayeed, MP

The Scots keep the Sabbath and everything else they can lay

their hands on.

The Welsh pray to God and on their neighbours.

The Irish don't know what they believe in, but will fight to the death to defend it.

And the English like to think of themselves as self-made men, thereby relieving the Almighty of a grave responsibility.

Anon

The President of the United States met the President of France and the Prime Minister of the UK.

'I'm in trouble,' said the President. 'I've [...] bodyguards and one of them is a member of the K[...] cannot find out which one it is.'

'My position is worse,' retorted the French Pres[...] have eighteen mistresses. One of them she is unfa[...] me. And I cannot find out which one it is.'

'My dilemma is worst of all,' said our Prime Mi[...] have eighteen people in my Cabinet. And one of [...] quite clever ... and I cannot find out which one it[...]

Malcolm Rifkind, MP

A definition of a diplomat is one who is disarming, [...] his country isn't!

Lord Aylestone, CH, CBE, PC

One evening in the late 1950s three Labour Membe[...] Parliament spoke at a public meeting in a school ha[...] in

Canton, Cardiff. Following the meeting and a lengthy question period, the three speakers, somewhat tired and quite hungry, decided to park the car in a side street to enjoy a hurried meal of fish and chips bought from a nearby shop.

The three speakers enjoying this succulent repast were:

James Callaghan – later to be Prime Minister.

George Thomas (now Lord Tonypandy), later to be Speaker of the House of Commons.

Bert Bowden (now Lord Aylestone), later to be Leader of the House of Commons, Lord President of the Privy Council and later still, Chairman of the Independent Broadcasting Authority.

Geoff Lawler, MP

An MP's life involves going to many dinners such as tonight's: for example, last week I was speaking at the Bradford Haemorrhoid Sufferers Society – a stand-up buffet; the week before that it was the Bolton Naturists' Group; the week before that I was invited to talk to the Idle Gay Rugby League Club Annual Dinner, and prior to that, the Eccleshill Ex-Convicts Association.

So for those of you who have heard this speech four times already this month, I apologise.

The Earl Haig, OBE, DL

An old Borderer with a good Scots accent once described an evening's fishing in the company of a friend with a wooden leg. It was nearly dark and the light was poor but the one-legged fisherman waded deeper to cover some good trout rising on the far side below a bank. Suddenly there was a tug and the fisher thought he was into a big one with that slow deliberate take that big fish are wont to make.

My Border friend described to me what happened: 'Unfortunately whote haad actually haapened was that the beesh wose a stirrk [bullock] and the flee was yoackit an ats baack – the stirrk muived yin staip, the fisherman muived as wail. Neither of them kenned whote haad haapened.' So on and on it went, the fisherman edging forward very deliberately determined not to lose the fish, and the stirk edging gradually into the darkness. The fisherman moved, the stirk moved. Again the fisherman moved, the stirk moved. This went on for some time until eventually the one-legged fisherman could wade no deeper and the 3lb breaking-strain cast was broken.

Luckily, the friend was near and able to explain what had happened, otherwise a very tall fishing story would have been told at home that night.

David Mudd, MP

Two MPs were calmly chopping an absent mutual friend to bits.

'What annoys me about him,' said the first, 'is that he has no modesty. He's a shrieking violet.'

'Yes,' agreed the other, 'he always minds his own business at the top of his voice.'

Lord Crathorne, DL

Some years ago two farmers in North Yorkshire went to court over a dispute they were having. The farmer with the

weaker case asked his solicitor if it would help if he sent the judge 'a couple of duck'. The solicitor replied that such an action would certainly lose him the case.

To the solicitor's surprise his client won the case. As soon as they were outside the courtroom the smiling farmer explained that he had in fact sent the judge a brace of duck. The solicitor was speechless with astonishment and after a short pause the farmer added, 'Aye, but I sent them in t'other man's name.'

Ken Hargreaves, MP

The person proposing a toast to the guests often finds it difficult when he knows little about them. When this happened recently to a colleague all that he knew about the chief guest was that he played golf at the local club. He rang the club to get as much information about him as he could.

'Oh, he's a war-time golfer,' said the Captain.

'What does that mean?'

'Out in 39, back in 45,' came the reply.

A. Cecil Walker, JP, MP

There was this guest speaker who was attending a function in Belfast where there were a lot of prominent politicians.

One of the problems was in giving the VIPs an opportunity to say a few words without the thing turning into a speech marathon. It was decided, therefore, to have each one of them talk for three minutes on the subject of 'Service'.

The first VIP talked about 'Service to the Public'; the next about 'Service to the Country' and so on. After more than half an hour of steady talk about 'Service', it was the guest speaker's turn to speak.

'When I was just a boy, my father had a registered bull and he was always being asked to rent the bull out for "Service" here and there. I was always curious to find out what all this "Service" was about, but my father kept putting me off, saying I was too young.

'One day my folks were in town and a neighbour sent over a message saying that he wanted to borrow the bull for a while. I figured that this would be my chance to find out what "Service" was, so I took the bull over to my neighbour.

'When I got there, the neighbour took the bull from me, thanked me for bringing him over and told me that I could go home and that he would bring the bull back himself. I told him that I wanted to stay and watch, but, just like my father, the neighbour told me I was too young.

'Well, I pretended to leave, but after a few minutes I sneaked back to the high board fence where they had taken the bull. Finally, I found a knothole. Well gentlemen, it was through that knothole in that high board fence that I saw what politicians have been doing to the people of Northern Ireland for the past fifteen years.'

John Scott
During coffee break the bank clerk heard how the milkman in his area had 'had' every woman in the street in which he lived, except one. When he confronted his wife with this news she said, 'I bet it's that miserable bitch in number 47.'

Harry Greenway, MP
Surgeon to patient after operation: 'First the bad news: we have removed the wrong leg. Next the good news: you haven't got gangrene.'

Cyril D. Townsend, MP

On one occasion the Irish writer Yeats addressed the Irish Senate on the subject of censorship. Encouraged by a crowded Chamber, he made one of the most effective speeches of his life, full of wit and wisdom, and showing a great knowledge of the religious and historical culture of his country.

When he had finished, an almost illiterate Senator stood up and said, 'Jaysus, Mr Yeats took the very words out of my mouth!'

Richard Ottaway, MP

A rather aged gentleman went into a well-established cobbler's shop in Nottingham and asked if the shoes which he had left for repair were ready.

The old man behind the counter enquired if the gentleman had a ticket, which he had, and which he handed over. It was a rather old ticket, and the man asked when the shoes had been handed in, to which the gentleman replied, 'Sometime in 1948.'

The cobbler retreated into the back room of the shop and was gone for about twenty minutes; he returned carrying a rather dusty pair of shoes and when he had blown off the dust, the gentleman said, 'Yes that's them, can I have them?'

The cobbler replied, 'They will be ready on Friday, sir.'

Greg Knight, MP

It came to pass that Neil Kinnock went to Heaven and he arrived at the Pearly Gates and said to St Peter, 'Can I come in?' whereupon St Peter said, 'Ah, now,' as he consulted a large book, 'well, according to my records, if you want to come into Heaven you are going to have to serve a penance and your penance will be to spend every night for the next three years with the lady over there, and he pointed out the most gruesome-looking creature, who looked as if she had just walked off the set of *Macbeth*. Neil Kinnock said, 'What, I can't do that, she's absolutely horrible. I'd rather go to Hell than that.' So St Peter said, 'Well, that's your choice,' and off Mr Kinnock went down to Hell. When he got there he found it occupied by Denis Healey, Harold Wilson and the Conservative Whips' Office so he decided he just couldn't take that and would rather suffer the awful penance awaiting him in Heaven.

He went back to St Peter and said, 'Now look, I have been thinking about this, can't I negotiate? Instead of all night for three years how about half a night for two years?' St Peter thought about it and said, 'Well, all right – you drive a hard bargain. The answer is yes.' Just then Neil Kinnock saw through the Gates of Heaven Anthony Wedgwood Benn walking arm in arm with Joan Collins. Neil Kinnock just couldn't believe it and said to St Peter, 'What in Heaven's name is going on; here I am the most popular Leader of the Labour Party for years, good-looking, intelligent, admired by all and there's Tony Benn, one of the most feared and divisive people in my party; how come he deserves that?' St Peter turned to him and said, 'Mr Kinnock, you just don't understand – he's Joan Collins's penance!'

Sir Kenneth Lewis, DL, MP

An Englishman in Paris was offered dinner, wine and a hostess for £25. He responded: 'The hostess can't be very good.'

Cyril D. Townsend, MP

During the time of President Idi Amin in Uganda, a judge arrived late for a banquet that was being given in a barracks by President Amin.

The short-sighted judge failed to find his name card on the table and finally plucked up courage and went over to one of the President's aides, 'Excuse me, but I cannot find my name on the table.'

The aide coolly looked up, 'Have you looked down the menu?'

Jonathan Sayeed, MP

'It's my job to talk and yours to listen. If you finish first, let me know.'

Roy Galley, MP

A mathematics teacher of mine at school uttered two lines in fairly rapid succession which became immortalised amongst us as schoolboys. On one occasion he was explaining a mathematical problem with the assistance of his blackboard and he said, 'Now watch this blackboard whilst I go through it.' This particular teacher did have some difficulty in keeping order in the class and a few days later he was heard to utter, 'Every time I open my mouth, some idiot speaks.'

The Bishop of Chichester

Dr R.R. Marett, former Rector of Exeter College, Oxford, was a great teller of tall stories. In his earlier days he had written a small pioneer work on Anthropology, published under that title by the Home University Library whose books in those days were isued at a shilling a volume. After it was published, somebody pointed out to Dr Marett a number of inaccuracies in it, to which Marett replied, 'Huh, can't expect the truth for a shilling.'

Sir John Biggs-Davison, MP

Some of us have difficulty in remembering funny stories:

A nervous young parliamentary candidate lacked confidence as a public speaker. So he asked a senior MP of his party for advice.

'Always try to make the audience laugh *with* you,' said the latter, 'then you'll get 'em on your side.' He gave an example: 'I often start like this:

' "Some of the happiest days of my life/Have been spent in the arms of another man's wife!" Then I pause for ten seconds while the audience gapes and gasps and occasionally titters. I continue with the punch line: "I refer, of course, to my mother." '

The Candidate thanked the Member and thought he would try it at his next public meeting. He started well enough:

'Some of the happiest days of my life
Have been spent in the arms of another man's wife.'

Then the dramatic pause. He let ten seconds pass ...

fifteen … twenty seconds. The audience breathed deeply and shifted uneasily in their seats. Finally, the Candidate stammered forth: 'But I'm damned if I can remember who she was.'

Lord Cullen of Ashbourne, MBE

A well-known conductor offered to perform at a concert in a remote country village. On arriving at the rehearsal he was warned that the first violinist had got 'flu but that they had borrowed a good violinist from a neighbouring village. He was, however, warned that though a pretty good violinist, this replacement was very scruffy in appearance.

At the start of the rehearsal the conductor looked sternly at the violinist and said, 'Do you know you've got your fly buttons undone?'

The violinist replied, 'Could you hum it?'

Tim Rathbone, MP

'The trouble with political jokes is that half of them get elected.'

'Nostalgia's all right; but it's not what it was.'

Chris Patten, MP

During General de Gaulle's State Visit to Britain in the late 1950s, Lady Dorothy Macmillan was given the job of escorting the General's wife while the official talks proceeded. This was no easy task since Madame de Gaulle

was short on charm and even shorter on jolly conversation.

Day after day Lady Dorothy took Madame de Gaulle to museums, Hampton Court, and so on, without getting much of a response.

On the last day of the visit it was decided that the two ladies should go for a spin in the country to see Beachy Head. They drove down through the English countryside with Lady Dorothy's increasingly frantic efforts to get a conversation going falling on very stony ground. Eventually, they got to Beachy Head and it was a glorious afternoon. Lady Dorothy jumped from the official Humber and walked briskly to the cliff's edge. She stared into the distance and then turned and came back to the car. 'Madame,' she said, 'you must get out and see the view. It is such a clear day. I believe you can see France.' Madame de Gaulle was unimpressed. She coughed bleakly and replied, 'Je l'ai déjà vu.'

Robert Atkins, MP

Young priest to doctor: 'Why is it that talking to God is praying, but when God talks to me it's called schizophrenia?'

Ron Brown, MP

During the General Election, I regularly spoke, using a loudspeaker, outside a large Leith factory to groups of employees. This was very popular, apparently confirmed by the fact that an old lady in a nearby house kept on waving to me on each occasion.

One day, near the end of the campaign, she rushed across

the road and grabbed my arm. 'Laddie,' she said. 'I've been trying tae catch ye' for weeks – can you no' shout quietly?'

Ken Thomas, Police Constable 630A, Members' Lobby
A school teacher asked for one of her class to tell a story with a moral.

Johnny told the story of his grandfather in the trenches during the war.

'All his mates had been killed, miss. He only had five bullets, a bayonet and a bottle of scotch. Lonely and afraid, he suddenly saw ten German soldiers creeping up to his trench. Grandad drank the scotch, shot five Germans dead, leapt from the trench, charged, and bayoneted the remaining five.'

'A very brave story, John, but what is the moral?'

'Don't mess about with my Grandad when he's drunk!'

Lord Jacobson, MC
As Henry VIII said to his wife, 'I won't keep you long …'

Hugh Dykes, MP
Letter to a Problem Page:

'Can you help me with my problem – I'm from a broken home, I suffer from an uncurable disease, my mother is an alcoholic, my father is in prison for embezzlement, my brother is a drug addict, I have a cousin in the SDP, I myself have been convicted three times for shoplifting, I have an uncle who has been doing seven years for GBH, my sister is

71

a notorious transvestite, and my grandfather has just been charged with indecent behaviour on a golf course.

'I am desperate and feeling suicidal, can you please, please help me. What *am* I going to do with my lousy rotten cousin who's in the SDP?'

Lord Davies of Leek, PC

My brother telephoned me one day to say his son was going to take his 'O' levels in Welsh, Woodwork and Scripture, and when I asked what all that was good for, he replied that his son would eventually like to set up as an undertaker, and all that would be very useful and good for business!

Cranley Onslow, MP

Three American clergymen discussing the question of when life begins. 'At the moment of conception,' says the Catholic. 'At the point of birth,' states the Episcopalian. 'You are both in error,' says the Rabbi. 'Life does not begin until the children leave home and the dog dies.'

Robin Corbett, MP

These 10 points from the Health Education Council booklet *Feeling Great* must be one of the best after-dinner stories ... depending on the audience, of course!:

1 GET MOVING – choose activities you really enjoy.
2 Make it regular – preferably three times a week.
3 Keep it up for at least 15 minutes a time.

4 Start gently and increase the effort gradually.
5 Get family or friends to join you.
6 Keep a watch on your weight – stay slim.
7 Cut down fatty foods – especially dairy products and meat.
8 Steady on the sugar and sweet things.
9 Eat more fibre – like brown bread or wholemeal bread, fruit, cereals and potatoes.
10 GET STARTED – NOW!

Roger Gale, MP

A Lieutenant-Colonel: 'Since our arrival in this city, fifteen of my soldiers have married local girls, fourteen of my soldiers have become engaged to local girls ...'

A voice from the audience: 'Stop while your still on top!''

Piers Merchant, MP

An illustration of the increasing dangers we, as a society, face from jargon-ridden professions and bureaucrats!

A Durham miner was unfortunately injured in a pit accident. He decided to sue the Coal Board and the case went to court. The hearing became increasingly technical and complicated, and eventually the issue revolved around the miner's own responsibility for the accident.

The judge was a learned expert on the law of damages, but possessed the other-worldliness reserved only for members of his profession. He had never talked to a miner, and was not even sure what they did down the pits. As the trial reached a climax the bewigged judge, with his polished cheeks and gold-rimmed glasses on the end of his nose, stopped the legal argument and peered hawkishly over the bench to the litigant. Fixing him with a glassy stare, he then turned to the man's barrister and said, 'Has not your client heard of the well-known legal maxim *non profitere se fit injuria?*'

Quick as a flash the barrister, better schooled in the language of the pit villages, replied, 'M'Lud, they talk of nothing else in the pubs and clubs of County Durham.'

The pit man was no wiser, but the language of the common man reigned supreme.

Greg Knight, MP

A politician who was feeling unwell went to his doctor who gave him an examination and then said, 'I've got bad news for you. You've got three minutes to live.'

The politician was devastated – 'Can't you do anything for me?' he cried.

'Well,' the Doctor answered. 'I can boil you an egg!'

Ivan Lawrence, QC, MP

Judge Maud sitting at the Old Bailey sentenced two homosexuals who had committed an indecent act under Waterloo Bridge with these words:

'It is not the enormity of the crime itself that appalls one. It is the fact that you chose to do it under one of London's most beautiful bridges.'

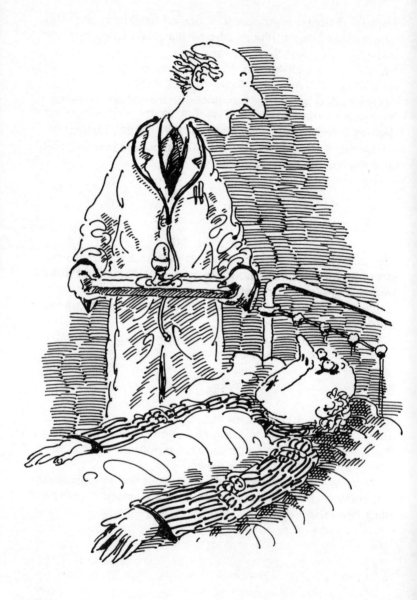

Lady Eyre (actress Anne Clements)

How's this for an introduction to your after-dinner speech?

'Anyone who has never heard Sir Reginald Eyre speak before will be looking forward to hearing him. I am sure you will enjoy his debatable qualities, and find his speech as moving as the food has been.'

Follow that!

Sir Reginald Eyre, MP

During Lloyd George's premiership in 1917 two French Ministers arrived at Downing Street to see him. Wishing to show particular consideration, Mrs Lloyd George walked into the drawing room to explain in French to the visitors the reason for her husband's delayed arrival.

'Pardon, messieurs,' she said with careful diction, 'Mon mari est dans le cabinet et je crois qu'il serra longtemps parce que il a pris beaucoup de papier avec lui.'

Steve Norris, MP

An Englishman, an Irishman and a Scotsman were walking on holiday in the Vatican gardens. As they turned a corner, they saw to their horror the unmistakable figure of the Pope lying prone before them. A hastily summoned cleric confirmed the Pontiff's demise and, obviously agitated, swore the three to silence until two or three days had lapsed in which a formal announcement could be made.

Musing over the extraordinary incident on the plane

home the next day, the Englishman suddenly hit on the idea that they could make a fortune by placing a large bet on the likelihood of the Pope being pronounced dead within the next week. They all agreed it was a first-class idea and agreed to meet in a few days to compare results.

A week later the Englishman stepped out of a new Rolls-Royce to meet the Scot emerging from a brand-new Mercedes. 'Well, I shall never work again,' said the Englishman. 'I got a thousand to one and laid on a thousand pounds.' 'I didn't do badly,' said the Scotsman, 'but not being so flush I only bet a hundred pounds.' Just then, the Irishman appeared alighting from a nearby bus. 'What happened to you?' they asked. 'I lost.' 'How could you possibly lose?' 'Well,' said the Irishman, 'I thought it was such a good idea, I did him in a double with the Archbishop of Canterbury.'

Lord Lloyd, MBE, DL

The Headmaster of a well-known public school decided that it was necessary to raise the school fees. So he wrote round to parents to say that the fees would have to be raised by £x per annum. Unfortunately his secretary omitted one of the n's so that it read 'per anum'. A friend of mine on receiving this missive wrote back and said that whilst regretting the rise in the fees, he would prefer to pay through the nose as before.

Lord Croft

A recently ennobled politician was asked by a waiter at a party what his name was. Indignant at not being recognised he exclaimed – 'My good man, don't you know it?'

The waiter replied dryly, 'I am afraid not, sir, but I will make enquiries!'

Cyril Smith, MBE, MP

Mrs Thatcher passes on – knocks on Gates of Heaven but St Peter, after enquiring her name sends her down below. Some four days later there is a knock on the Gates of Heaven – St Peter goes and finds the Devil standing there. 'What do you want,' asks St Peter.

'Oh,' says the Devil, 'I've come to seek political asylum!'

John Wakeham, PC, MP

The story I remember best from my time at the Treasury was overhearing two Treasury Mandarins discussing a tricky problem; one said: 'That's OK in practice, but what's wrong with it in theory?'

Edwina Currie, MP

The problems with a lady politician all revolve around credibility. You see, if a politicians says 'yes' we know he means 'maybe'. If he says 'maybe' he probably means 'no'. But if he says 'no' then he's not a politician.

However, when a lady says 'no', we recognise that she means 'maybe'. And when she says 'maybe' she probably means 'yes'. But if she says 'yes', then she's no lady …

– so what am I to do?

Lord Colwyn

When flying on a particularly long journey, the late Arthur Askey called one of the hostesses to ask if he could see some of the magazines.

When asked which magazine he would like to read, he replied 'The *National Geographic Magazine*, please.'

'I'm awfully sorry,' replied the hostess, 'we don't have that with us. Is there another one I can get for you instead?'

'How about *Playboy*?' said Arthur, after a little thought.

'Oh dear,' said the hostess, 'that's another one we don't have on this flight, I am sorry.'

After a short pause the hostess's curiosity got the better of her and she said, 'Tell me, sir, why did you ask for two so totally different magazines?'

'That's easy,' said Arthur, 'I really love looking at the places I'm never likely to go to.'

David Sumberg, MP

Shortly after being elected, I had to visit a well-known girls' boarding school in order to talk to them about my experience as a new Member. Because of the distance involved, I had to stay overnight at the school; dropping off to sleep that night in my lonely bed, I was much comforted by the notice over my bed which read 'Please ring the bell if you need a mistress in the night'.

Cyril D. Townsend, MP

During the premiership of Lord Salisbury a spot of trouble occurred in the Persian Gulf. The Prime Minister gave the Admiralty orders to send a gunboat and asked for the commander of the gunboat to report to him before he sailed.

During the course of his briefing the commander asked what he was to do if the natives in the area did not yield to the threat offered by the gunboat's arrival.

Lord Salisbury replied, 'Get up steam and leave.'

A few weeks later the gunboat arrived in the area, and its commander had an interview with the obdurate Sultan who said to him, 'Commander, I have patiently listened to you, you must now tell me what happens if we refuse to meet your unreasonable terms.'

The commander replied, 'Reluctantly, you will leave me with no alternative, but to carry out the second part of my orders.'

There was a pause, then the Sultan gave in.

Nicholas Baker, MP

We all know the story about the member of the House of Lords who dreamt once that he was making a speech in the House of Lords and woke up to find that he was!

David Amess, MP

The day after the election many Members took to the sunny

roads for the last time; the general idea being to drive leisurely around the constituency thanking all those who had voted for them.

It was a beautiful day as I stood in the open-top car using the loud-hailer to thank all and sundry for putting me into Parliament for the first time. The atmosphere was so euphoric that upon passing through the only upmarket farming section of the constituency I even had a word for the animals.

To one herd of cows I said very loudly and very distinctly, 'I should like to thank the cows of Bowers Gifford for voting Conservative.' The herd turned as one to peer at the disturber of the peace. Chuckling, I turned to face the road, only to see four or five very Conservative-looking ladies staring directly at me with *no* trace of amusement on their faces!

Susan Ketelsen

In 1979 the Secretary of State for Defence was about to speak at a public meeting in a by-election in Manchester, a place famed for its two football clubs. The Chairman's opening remarks were fairly brief, just indicating how fortunate we were to have a Cabinet Minister and concluded, 'Ladies and Gentleman, will you please welcome Francis Lee.' Francis Pym beamed. 'Francis Lee, former Manchester City and England forward.'

Jeremy Hanley, MP

It is always difficult to know how long to make a speech, but the best advice came from the Bishop of Southwark who in opening his sermon said that at Theological College he was

taught two rules about sermons. 'Preach about Christ and preach about twenty minutes.'

John Watson, MP

In early December last year I went along to speak at the Annual General Meeting of the Pateley Bridge Branch of the Conservative Party.

I mentioned to the Chairman that December seemed an unusual time for a branch to hold its AGM – most branches seek to have such meetings in October.

'We did have a meeting in October,' he replied, 'but only six people turned up so we decided to hold it again tonight with a bit of an incentive for people to come.'

'I see,' I said, 'and is that why I am your speaker tonight?'

'No, it's not. We've laid on some crisps and a meat pie.'

Lord Flowers

Crash programmes are of doubtful value. They remind me of the man who attempted to get nine women pregnant in the hope of producing one infant in one month.

Nicholas Lyell, QC, MP

At the time we married, my wife was teaching in an infant and junior school in Pimlico. In the classroom, they had a tank containing a goldfish, and one day the goldfish (as is their wont) died. This was noted by the children with much sadness and that evening after school my wife went to the local market and bought another goldfish, which she popped into the tank next morning. When the children arrived for class, one little boy saw the goldfish in the tank. He looked at it for a moment, then turned to my wife, his eyes bright with admiration. 'Hey, miss,' he said, 'you've got 'im workin' again!'

Tim Renton, MP

A true story that happened to me while canvassing in Sheffield on a hot June evening in 1970:

In Sheffield the tradition is that the front door is reserved for wakes and weddings. Candidates therefore go round to the back door. I did so and found myself looking in through the window at a burly steel-worker who was soaking himself down in the bath. Embarrassed, I looked away at his garden and saw it was full of primroses.

'I see you've got lots of primroses,' I said.

'Aye,' he commented.

'Did you know primroses were Disraeli's favourite flower?' I asked.

'Is that so?' he replied. 'In that case I'll dig the buggers up tomorrow.'

Gary Waller, MP

A chap from out of town was visiting London for the first time when he was attacked by muggers not far from the House of Commons. After knocking him about and robbing him of all his possessions, they left him bleeding and lying in the gutter.

Soon after, a Conservative MP came by and noticing the man in the gutter, crossed the street to see what was wrong.

'Goodness,' he said, 'you need help, my man!' and went away to telephone, praying that the ambulance had not been axed in the Government's spending cuts.

A moment or two later, a Labour MP came along, and likewise went to investigate. 'My God!' he said. 'Whoever did this to you needs help.'

Seconds after he had gone, a Liberal MP appeared on the scene. 'Quick!' he said. 'Tell me what the other two said to you!'

Edwina Currie, MP

This story should be told in a broad Derbyshire accent:

A woman MP is generally expected to look nice at functions, and not disgrace herself by sliding under the table. But I struck a unique problem at a farmers' dinner recently.

We were celebrating the extension of a local animal feeds mill, the owner of which laid on a splendid blow-out at the local hostelry. Conscious of the need to counteract the expansionary tendencies of my figure, I was a little careful of what I ate; no bread, no butter, no potatoes; a fruit juice instead of the locally brewed ale; no pudding. But it was as I started to put a saccharine tablet in my (black) coffee, that an old farmer sitting opposite, who had been watching me with increased suspicion, leaned across the table and protested, 'You may be my MP, Mrs Currie, but you ain't eaten anything yet that I grow!'

Lord Davies of Leek, PC

A farmer I knew was out walking when he came across a lad with a lighted lantern in his hand, who, when asked where he was going, said that he was going up the mountain to do some courting. The farmer then said that when he was a boy he didn't go courting with a lighted lantern, whereat the lad replied, 'When I see what your missus looks like, it might have been better if you had!'

Anon

The Chairman of the 1922 Committee (the committee of back-bench Tory MPs) was seated in his office recently when his secretary said the Prime Minister was on the line. All the secretary heard from him was, 'No, no, no, yes, no. Goodbye.'

'Well you certainly told her,' said the Secretary, 'but what was the "Yes"?'

'Oh,' he said, 'she just asked me if I was still listening.'

Ted Rowlands, MP

I recall the first time that I attempted to leglislate in 1966. The whole of the committee stage of the Finance Bill used to be taken on the Floor of the House and often we would sit until the middle of the night. The Labour Party was in Government, and I remember one night going into the Chamber and seeing six Opposition spokesmen, one Whip, and my Right Honourable Friend the Member for Cardiff, South and Penarth (Mr Callaghan), then Chancellor of the Exchequer. There was no one else on our side. I thought, 'This is disgraceful – where is the Government support?' So I sat and listened to the debate. I could not resist the temptation to intervene.

I intervened two or three times with growing confidence, only to be the target of more and more glum looks from the

Chancellor of the Exchequer. Eventually, a note was passed to me saying, 'What do you think you are doing?' What I was doing was self-evident – I was taking part in the great thrust of democratic debate. I wrote on the note 'Legislating' and sent it back. In a flash another note returned saying: 'Don't!'

Greg Knight, MP

An inexperienced Irishman was elected a shop steward and very soon announced to his members that, after meeting the management, he had some good news and some bad news to give to them.

'Give us the bad news first,' shouted one of the brothers.

'The bad news, my friends, is that due to the lack of orders, I have been forced to negotiate with the management a wage cut of 10%, but,' he continued, 'the good news is that I have persuaded the management to back-date this for six months.'

Peter Archer, PC, QC, MP

When the first Roman Legion came to Britain, they were marching along the Birmingham-Wolverhampton road, and had just reached Birchley Bus Garage, when a head emerged from the trees and shouted: 'Yah, one Black Countryman's worth ten Romans.'

The Commander, determined to teach the locals a lesson, immediately despatched ten men into the trees. There was the sound of body crashing against body, the noise of blows, cries of pain, and then – silence! They never saw the Romans again.

A moment later the head re-appeared. 'What did I tell

you? One Blackcountryman's worth fifty Romans.' Deciding that this had gone far enough, the Commander despatched fifty crack fighting troops after his tormentor. The noise and the cries continued longer this time. Then there was silence. No more Romans.

The head re-appeared. 'See – one Blackcountryman's worth a hundred Romans.' The honour of Imperial Rome was at stake. The Commander instructed a Centurion to take a crack unit of a hundred men, and not to return until the problem was finally settled. This time, the noise and the cries continued for quite a long time. Then there emerged from the trees a solitary Roman, battered and bleeding.

He managed to gasp, 'It was a trick. There was an ambush. There were two of them!'

Tony Speller, MP

On referring to one of his opponents in a General Election: 'Here is one who only opens his mouth to change feet.'

Richard Tracey, JP, MP

As a former broadcaster and press man I have often wondered about the origin of the public relations man. I recently discovered it:

Apparently when Moses was leading his people out of Egypt he arrived at the rather daunting barrier of the Red Sea. The screaming hordes of their pursuers were close behind. Somewhat desperately, he looked at the wide expanse of waters and said, 'If only I could hold up my arm now and call upon these waters to part ...'

A little chap who was standing next to him quickly said, 'My goodness, sir, if you could do that I could guarantee to

get you four pages in the Old Testament.'

The origins of the slick public relations operator are obviously deep.

John Lee, MP, Under-Secretary of State for Defence Procurement

On having made it clear to his inquisitive daughters, Deborah (8) and Elspeth (6), that on no account must they go into his ministerial box, he received the plea: 'But daddy, we're only children – we won't tell the Germans the war secrets.'

John Hannam, MP

An English judge went over to Ireland to take assizes. A case was brought before him in which Paddy Murphy was accused of stealing three sheep. The evidence was clear cut and the judge summed up before despatching the jury to make its judgement. When they returned the foreman was asked for the verdict and he said, 'Not guilty M'Lud.' – The judge was horrified at this ridiculous verdict and sent them back to reconsider – which they did for an hour. On their return it was the same story, 'Not guilty, M'Lud.' The Judge then patiently explained that there was no possibility of such a travesty of justice being acceptable to him and they must reconsider the evidence again. This time the jury was out for two hours and when they returned the foreman was asked to give the verdict. In a trembling voice he said, 'Not guilty, M'Lud, so long as he returns the three sheep.'

Lord Chalfont, OBE, MC, PC

A distinguished Foreign Office official, now an equally distinguished member of the House of Lords, was, in his early days as a diplomat, officiating as Resident Clerk at the Foreign Office. The function of the Resident Clerk is to occupy a small flat in the Foreign and Commonwealth Office at night and over the weekend, and to deal with any crisis which might arise when the rest of the office is closed. In the course of one otherwise uneventful weekend, the Resident Clerk received in the early hours of Sunday morning a cable from a Middle Eastern post which contained the simple plea 'RULER HAS DIED SUDDENLY. PLEASE ADVISE.'

After pondering for a moment, the young official drafted a telegram of reply and went back to sleep. The telegram said quite simply 'HESITATE TO DOGMATISE, BUT SUGGEST BURIAL.'

Alastair Goodlad, MP

Prolix Minister, on finding public meeting sparsely attended: 'Chairman, was this meeting widely publicised?'

Chairman: 'No, Minister, but I fear that there must have been a departmental leak.'

John Fraser MP

Scene – MP at surgery.

1st Constituent: 'I'm being followed each night from work

by a spy who gets on the train at Earl's Court. What can I do?'

MP: 'I think you may be a bit paranoiac – but of course that doesn't mean that people aren't getting at you.'

1st Constituent: 'Suggest something!'

MP: 'Well, every night when you leave work buy a newspaper, fold it and tear a small hole in the fold and then use it as a spy hole to look at people on the tube. When the man following you realises he's been rumbled he will stop following you.'

1st Constituent: 'Thanks – I'll try.'

A week later –

1st Constituent: 'Thanks – I've tried it and it works.'

Two weeks later –

2nd Constituent: 'I'm being followed each night from work by a man with a spy hole in a newspaper ...'

Robert Atkins, MP

Statistics prove anything. In London traffic one man is knocked down every fifteen minutes – and he's getting pretty fed up with it!

Robert Banks, MP

Some time ago I was discussing the problems Members of Parliament have in arriving at meetings on time with an eminent Italian MP.

I explained that on one occasion my wife and I were driving up to my constituency in Yorkshire for my Annual General Meeting. While I was travelling at some speed, a pheasant crossed the road. I could not avoid it and hit it full

on. I continued my journey. Some time later we were stopped by traffic lights and my wife persuaded me to check the front of the car to see what damage might have been done. To my horror I found that one headlamp had been smashed and there was blood on the wing of the car.

I then pulled into a garage and was able to obtain a replacement lamp and have it fitted to the car.

Meantime, I telephoned the Chairman of the meeting and explained my predicament. However, by dint of fast driving we arrived at the meeting in time to make my speech.

My Italian friend remarked that it must have been an awful experience for me and then asked, 'Did you ever manage to find out what happened to the peasant?'

Cyril D. Townsend, MP

An Englishman's attitude abroad is always a subject of wonder to the locals. A few years ago an English banker had the misfortune to be buried in an earthquake in Turkey.

Sensing the approach of some rescuers he called out, 'Hi, pick me out first – I'm English, dammit! We're not used to this sort of thing.'

David Mitchell, MP

While electioneering near Andover in the last General Election, I knocked on the door of a house, which was opened by an attractive young housewife, and explained that I was the Conservative candidate and thought voters liked to meet the man they were asked to vote for.

At that moment she was joined by a beautiful red setter. I leant forward, patted the dog and continued: 'Aren't you lovely, aren't you beautiful. I would like to take you home with me.' There then occurred a minor explosion from behind a curtain and the husband of the household emerged, not having appreciated that I was addressing the dog and not his wife.

The Earl Amherst

A Senior Staff Officer at British GHQ in Cairo during the Second World War was concerned at what seemed to be unnecessary delays in the delivery of signals. He asked the Signalling Sergeant; 'I am a signal. I have just come in. What happens to me now?' The Sergeant answered: 'Sorry, sir, you'll have to go out and come in again – in triplicate.'

Greg Knight, MP

Two Frenchmen, who were visiting England for a short holiday, were anxious to 'do what the British do' whilst they were enjoying their stay in the United Kingdom. Knowing that most Englishmen prefer 'a pint' they decided that they would forgo their regular tipple of wine and would instead drink pints. However, they were not familiar with the name of any English beer and weren't sure how to place their order without showing their ignorance.

On arriving in London they noticed a hoarding on the side of a hotel which read 'Drink Epsom Salts and feel younger'. That, they decided, was to be their drink. On entering the hotel, the barman was a little surprised to receive an order for two pints of Epsom Salts, but the hotel being a five-star establishment, he complied without demurring.

Some ten pints later, they both decided they'd had enough. 'Well, Pierre,' said one. 'Do you feel any younger?'

His friend replied, 'Well, I don't know about that, but I've just done a very childish thing.'

Lord Constantine of Stanmore, CBE, AE, DL
A music lover is one who when told that Raquel Welch sings in the bath, puts his ear to the keyhole.

Patrick Nicholls, MP
The Western Area Office of the Conservative Party keeps a list of speakers who are prepared to go to outlandish places at short notice. Some years ago I was anxious to extend my speaking experience, and it was suggested to me that I might go on the Western Area list. Within 48 hours they had provided me with my first engagement, which was to address a meeting in a small village in one of the remoter parts of Cornwall. I was impressed by how quickly they had provided me with my first engagement but the significance of it did not strike me at the time.

To ensure that I arrived in good time for this most important engagement I left early, but everything went wrong. I got lost and then my car broke down.

When I finally arrived, three-quarters of an hour late, I sprinted into the hall, which was packed. The Chairman had obviously been having some trouble keeping the audience in order. However, even before I had removed my coat, he was introducing me. 'Ladies and Gentlemen, he has arrived. I know how pleased you will all be to hear him. Ladies and Gentlemen, Tony Speller.'

Richard Holt, MP

Did you hear about the Irish Paddy who ran into his friend Mick, who said, 'Hallo I've not seen you for some time, where have you been?'

'In jail.'

'Goodness, what was it like?'

'Sure, Mick, it was just like being on holiday.'

Two weeks later Mick was charged with serious breach of the peace, being drunk and disorderly, and smashing shop windows. The magistrate looked at him reprovingly and said, 'For such an offence there must be a custodial sentence.'

'Does that mean jail?' asks Mick.

'Yes,' says the magistrate.

'In which case,' says Mick, 'will you make it the last week in July and the first week in August.'

Jonathan Sayeed, MP

When making a weekly walkabout in my constituency I was made to realise how firmly the famous member from whom I inherited the seat was fixed in people's minds. I knocked on one door to be greeted by a particularly deaf elderly lady with thick pebble glasses. 'Good afternoon,' I said clearly, 'I'm your local MP, Jonathan Sayeed.' 'Oh,' she replied, grasping my hand, 'Mr Benn, how nice to meet you; you don't look half as daft as they say.'

Sir Reginald Eyre, MP

An old story has it that Sir Winston Churchill was visiting a parachute factory when he absentmindedly took out a cigar. The fire officer rushed up to him saying, 'Sir Winston, you mustn't smoke.'

'Oh, don't worry, dear boy, I don't inhale.'

John Browne, MP

On a wet and windy day during the General Election of 1979, whilst accompanied by other canvassers, I knocked on the door of a house near Andover. It was about twelve noon. I was greeted by a girl dressed in a very light-weight nightdress. As she reached out of the door to shake my hand, her foot came out of the doorway and the front door closed behind her. She had no key and the heavy rain was making her nightdress progressively more 'see-through'. I lent her my overcoat and noticed a window open on the first floor. At last we managed to break into her father's garage and pull out a ladder up which I climbed to the window, on to her bed and downstairs to let her in. The steeplejack activities certainly prevented the loss of at least one voter.

Later that evening in the Andover Conservative Club, a couple at the bar asked how my day had been and I related the story only to discover that I was talking to the parents of the girl in question. On this fortunate occasion, Mother was amused!

John Butterfill, MP

A Texan tourist is visiting Dorset, driving an enormous Cadillac motor car, the type with fins at the back and what looks like rocket exhausts.

On passing through a village, he notices an elderly countryman mowing the village green with an extra-ordinarily ancient mowing machine which looks as though it properly belonged in the Science Museum.

The American stops his car and the two eye each other without speaking for some minutes. Eventually the old countryman can contain his curiosity no longer and pointing to the Cadillac says to the American, 'What be that you got there?'

The American replies, 'Why, this, this is just a little automobile, but say, what is that you have got there?' (pointing to the mowing machine).

'This, why, this ought-to-mow grass, but it don't.'

Michael Blond

A new MP was desperate to get some television coverage and approached all the TV stations telling them he was available to talk about absolutely anything at any time of day or night. Eventually he received a letter from a TV company asking if he could appear on a particular programme and if a fee of £50 would be acceptable. He wrote back by return: 'I accept. My cheque for £50 is enclosed.'

Sir John Biggs-Davison, MP

A small boy came up to visit London and stay with his aunt. When he arrived at King's Cross they got into a taxi. They were driving round the corner when the small boy said – 'What are those ladies standing on the pavement for?' The aunt replied that they were waiting for their husbands. 'Why not tell the boy the truth?' said the taxi-driver, 'they are prostitutes.' The boy then asked if prostitutes have babies. 'Yes,' replied the aunt, 'where do you think taxi-drivers come from?'

Simon Coombes, MP

A young candidate was canvassing in a rural area not far from my constituency, and came upon a rather crusty old farmer ploughing a field with an equally crusty old horse.

'Good afternoon, sir,' said our young candidate, 'I am standing as the Conservative candidate in the local elections, and am wondering if I shall have your support?'

The farmer squinted and rubbed his chin. 'Arr,' he replied. 'Don't know 'bout that then! Me dad didn't vote, me granddad didn't vote, and what's good enough for them's good enough for me.'

At this point the candidate was trying desperately to keep the conversation going. 'I am very interested in your method of ploughing, sir. Do you prefer to use a horse, or have you ever thought of getting a tractor?'

'Arr,' he replied. 'Don't know 'bout that then! Me dad didn't 'ave a tractor, me granddad didn't 'ave a tractor, and what's good enough for them's good enough for me.'

Seeing that he was clearly getting nowhere with the old

man, and noticing a light in the window of the farmer's cottage, the young candidate asked, 'Thank you very much for your time, sir. I was wondering if I could go up to your house and talk to your wife? Perhaps she might be interested in supporting my campaign?'

The old farmer got very thoughtful and rubbed his chin. 'Arrr!' he said. 'Don't know 'bout that then! Oi don't 'ave a wife.'

'Oh, I see,' said the young candidate.

'Naw … Me dad didn't 'ave a wife, me granddad didn't 'ave a wife, and what's good enough for them's good enough for me!'

The Viscount Eccles, KCVO, PC

I took trouble with my maiden speech in the House of Commons (1943). It seemed to go well, but after I sat down Jimmy Maxton, an Independent Labour MP whom I had met at Nancy Astor's, came and gave me this advice:

'David, my boy, dinna put too much meat in your pie.'

K. Harvey Proctor, MP

I was invited to a school theatre group performance of *The Snow Queen*. I sat at the back of the room with the headmistress and the local Education Officer while the five-, six- and seven-year-old children sat crossed-legged on the floor – all but one young girl watching the production avidly. This young lady kept looking round at me throughout the entire performance and at the end, when she stood up to go back to the school classroom, she turned to me, looked up at me and said, 'I know who you are.'

'Oh, yes,' I said, 'and who do you think I am?'
'You're Flash Gordon,' she replied.

Greg Knight, MP

A left-wing feminist MP was addressing a number of her colleagues on the evils of smoking.

'I have been an MP for over five years and have never put a cigarette between my lips,' she ranted.

Overhearing this, an old boy responded, 'Madam, I have been an MP for twenty-five years and have never put one anywhere else.'

Lord Jacobson, MC

'Sit still, Johnnie,' said the teacher. But Johnnie kept on shuffling.

'What's the matter with you?' asked the teacher.

'Please, miss, I was circumcised yesterday, I cannot sit still.'

'Go to the headmaster,' said the teacher.

Ten minutes later Johnnie returned with the offending piece of his anatomy sticking out of his trousers.

'You disgusting hateful boy,' said the teacher. 'Have you seen the headmaster?'

'Yes, miss, he told me to stick it out until the lunch break.'

Lord Thomson of Fleet

A London antique dealer was very knowledgeable in his field but naive and inexperienced in other areas, for he

seldom left London and then only to travel occasionally to country auctions. He had never travelled abroad in his life. He was accustomed to having lunch every day at the same club, at the same time and with the same dealer friends.

One day a special sale came up in Paris which offered such an array of potential goods for his shop that he simply had to make the trip to Paris to bid for the objects himself. His friends wondered how in Heaven's name he would ever make out in a strange country, never having travelled before, not speaking the French language and not ever having had any experience of this kind.

When he returned from Paris they were anxious to find out how he had got on.

'Oh, I got along extremely well,' said the dealer, 'I had no trouble at all.'

His dealer friends were nonplussed. 'But you don't speak the language and you have never travelled before in a foreign country. How did you manage it?'

'Oh, there are ways and means,' the dealer said. 'I found I didn't really need to know how to *speak* French at all. For instance, I met an attractive young lady one afternoon and immediately we seemed to hit it off nicely even though she did not speak English, nor I French. After a few minutes I took my pencil and pad out of my pocket and drew a picture of a park with a bench. She caught on immediately and we went to the park and sat on a bench in the sun and watched the world go by.

Later on I took my pencil and pad out again and drew a picture of a theatre and she again caught on immediately. We walked along to a theatre and went in and enjoyed the play.

After the performance was over I took my pencil and pad again and drew a picture of a place-setting with wine glasses – she understood at once and we went to a lovely restaurant and had a most enjoyable dinner together.

But then a strange thing happened. She grabbed the pencil and pad and drew a picture of a four-poster bed.

Now how on earth do you suppose she ever figured out that I was an antique dealer?'

Cyril D. Townsend, MP

During the early days of British rule in Kenya, a European foreman in charge of a gang of Kikuyu labourers had a glass eye.

To keep his labourers working when he went off for his rather lengthy lunch each day, he took out his glass eye and left it on a post to watch over them.

Over-awed by the White Man's magic, they toiled hard in the heat of the day. But one day, one labourer, brighter than the rest, crept up behind the post and put his hat over the glass eye.

When the foreman returned he found the labourers sleeping soundly.

Sydney Chapman, MP

I was the only architect in the Commons when I lost my Birmingham seat in February 1974. I concluded my speech of thanks to my supporters, after the declaration, by saying that I could claim to be the only failed politician who could say literally: 'Ah, well, back to the drawing board.'

Archie Hamilton, MP

Man, driving home at night after an extremely good dinner, doing over 100 mph down the dual-carriageway in his new white Rover, notices that he is being followed by another white Rover.

110

Too late, he suddenly realises that the white Rover has an orange stripe down the side and a blue light on top. The siren wails.

'Will you get out of the car, sir, and blow into this bag?'

He lurches to his feet and is about to comply with the request when two cars crash into each other on the opposite carriageway. The police hurry across the road to take details.

Thinking quickly, our friend leaps into the car and drives off home at speed.

3 o'clock in the morning. He is woken by a hammering on the door, and with a splitting headache and frightful hangover goes to open it. It is the police.

'Were you stopped earlier this evening on the dual-carriageway?'

'No.'

'Well, do you mind if we inspect your car?'

'No, of course not, officer.'

On opening the garage door they see a white Rover, with an orange stripe down the side and a blue light on the top.

Lord Aylestone, PC, CH, CBE

It was said of a Cabinet Minister that he was such a good Minister that he would gladly travel from one end of the country to another 'To open an umbrella'.

Greg Knight, MP

I like the story about the MP who went away to a conference and, in the hotel foyer, he met a young lady who seemed quite keen on him. They went into the Reception and signed in as Mr and Mrs Smith for the night.

The next day the MP came downstairs, after breakfast in

bed and was presented for a bill for £500. He complained to the manager, 'Look, I have only stayed here one night.'

'Yes, sir,' the manager said, 'but your wife has been staying here for six weeks.'

'Moral: 'If you can't be good – be careful.'

Gary Waller, MP

Calling to see a farmer, a visitor could not help noticing something odd about one of the pigs. 'That's a fine lot of pigs you've got there,' he said, 'but tell me, why has that one there got a wooden leg?'

'Well,' replied the farmer, 'a month ago we had a fire. That pig rushed into the farmhouse, grabbed an extinguisher, got the fire under control, dragged my wife into the open air, and telephoned the fire brigade. When they got here, they found their job already done.'

'That's a remarkable story,' said the visitor. 'And that's a very remarkable pig! But you haven't told me why it has got a wooden leg.'

'A week after we had the fire,' explained the farmer, 'a burglar broke into the farmhouse while my wife and I were out. He bundled all our silver into a sack, and was about to ravish my daughter. Fortunately the pig heard the noise, crept up behind the intruder, hit him over the head with a vase and telephoned the police. When they arrived, the man was laid out on the floor, and all they had to do was to snap the handcuffs on and take him away.'

'That pig,' said the visitor, 'is the cleverest animal I've ever come across! But you still haven't told me why it has a wooden leg.'

'Come on now, be fair,' retorted the farmer, 'do you really think the wife and I would have had the heart to eat it all at once after everything it had done for us?'

Lord Caccia, GCMG, GCVO

A Minister on the Apple and Pear Development Council replying to a supplementary question said that so far as the Cox's Orange Pippin was concerned, he had recently heard of a friend of a friend who had an idea: He was going to do a little advertising on his own in France for that particular apple. He would take an aeroplane across the Channel and on it he would have individual Cox's apples with little parachutes on them on which would be printed a message that read: 'Every little French tart deserves an English Cox.'

John Mulkern, Managing Director, British Airports Authority

The Personnel Officer at a certain airport has a sure-fire method of putting recruits into the most appropriate section of the airport. He puts each recruit on his own for 15 minutes in a room equipped with only a chair, a newspaper and a TV set. After 15 minutes the Personnel Officer goes into the room to make the job assignment. If the candidate is standing at the window looking up at the sky, he is assigned to the Airfield Operations Unit. If he is scribbling on the walls, he is given a clerical job. If he is dismantling the inside of the TV set, he is assigned to Engineering. If he doesn't look up at all when the Personal Officer enters, he is made a security guard. If he is standing on the chair shouting and waving his arms, he is made Shop Steward and, if he cannot be found at all, he is made a Duty Officer.

Lord Chalfont, OBE, MC, PC

A distinguished American business man of somewhat advanced years, on retirement from his Board of Directors, bought a large house on the Eastern seaboard. The house was situated on a cliff-side overlooking the ocean, and one evening the old gentleman was out for his usual walk before going to bed. The evening was a very blustery one and when he ventured a little too near the brink of the cliff he lost his footing and fell over the brink. Fortunately he was able as he fell to grasp a very slender sapling which was growing out of the cliff, and arrest his fall. The old gentleman hung there for a few moments, terribly shaken, and then looking up he called out, 'Is there anybody there?'

All at once a great voice seemed to fill the whole of the firmament. It came out of the clouds and out of the sea and out of the cliff itself and it said in measured tones, 'There is always someone up here, my son. All that you need to do is to release your hold upon that small tree and you will descend safely to the shore below.'

The old gentleman considered this for a moment and looked down at the jagged rocks 200 feet below. Then he looked up again and said, 'Is there anybody *else* up there?'

Peter Sanguinetti, Director, Public Affairs, British Airports Authority

Whilst making an after-dinner speech in Strasbourg following an acrimonious debate on noise, a senior Italian official of DG X1 was interrupted by one of his political adversaries, who heckled 'Why have they introduced laws to stop helicopters flying over Rome?' The speaker's jaw fell, but he was saved from an embarrassing silence by someone else who retorted 'Because they go wop wop wop'.

William F. Newton Dunn, MEP
A limerick ascribed to US President Woodrow Wilson:

My face did not make me a star:
Others are fairer by far.
But I do not mind it
Because I am behind it;
It's you who're in front feel the jar.

Sir John H. Osborn, MP
Many years ago, when I was driving from the State of Victoria to Sydney I arranged, on leaving Albury, to call on the Mayor of Holbrook, named after an uncle of mine, my name being John Holbrok Osborn.

As I passed through Albury and stopped at the traffic lights, I learned to my cost that one should keep the passenger door locked. A typical Australian 'digger' leapt into the car and asked: 'Going North, mate?'

I had really no option but to drive him a few hundred yards on his way and explain that I was going North but was stopping at Holbrook for lunch.

He agreed to leave the car at Holbrook but asked me to guarantee that if later on in the afternoon I found him walking up the Hume Highway, please to pick him up and take him on his way to Wollongong, where he was a shop convener. He was satisfied that a 'Pommy' would keep his word, and in return he agreed to give me dinner at the far end of our journey – the old town of Bowral.

Sure enough later that afternoon, there was this 'digger'

tramping along the highway. I stopped, picked him up, and we chatted merrily until, while going round a bend he suddenly said to me, 'Mate, whatever you do, don't stop.'

My reply was to the effect that I saw no reason why I should want to stop, but then I saw a beautiful blonde with a low neckline trying to change a wheel because of a flat tyre, and inevitably I started to slow down.

'Mate, what did I tell you, don't stop.'

So against my better judgement we drove on and then he said, 'Mate, do you see those two old girls with howlin' kids in their perambulators?'

I said: 'Yes.'

'You would have stopped, wouldn't you?'

I said: 'Yes.'

'And they would have parked one perambulator in front of your car and one behind your car, and you wouldn't have had the heart to send one of those kids flying out of a perambulator, would you?'

'I reluctantly replied: 'No.'

Then he said as we drove on. 'See those caravans and those men with beards over there?'

And as I drove by I duly acknowledged: 'Yes.'

'Well, you would have been stuck between those two perambulators, eyeing that Moll, and before you knew what had happened to you, your car, your money, your wallet, your passport, your clothes and your suitcase would have been taken from you, wouldn't they?'

Reluctantly I conceded that this might have been the case.

'And you would have been left sitting on the side of the highway, wouldn't you?'

And again I reluctantly admitted: 'Yes.'

'And,' he said, 'no one would have stopped for you, for after all I am proof of that as no one picked me up since I started walking from Holbrook.'

Reluctantly I agreed: 'Yes.'

Finally the 'digger' asserted: 'Then, I think you have had such a let-off, mate, that when we get to Bowral, instead of me buying you a meal you should buy me one.'

That is how, several decades ago, an Australian hitch-hiker managed to talk himself into a lift off me for several hundred miles, and then talked me into willingly agreeing to buy him a good dinner.

Cyril D. Townsend, MP

An elderly Peer was forced to attend a major debate in the House of Lords facing downwards. A colleague commiserated with him but the elderly Peer replied, 'I can assure you, Sir, I have heard some of the nicest things ever said to me in this position.'

John Cope, MP

The self-made millionaire lay on his death-bed and sent for his son. 'My boy, I've done everything I could to give you a good start in life – good school, university, and now you have qualified as a chartered accountant. But I believe a man should make his own money. Promise me you will bury all my money in my coffin with me.' The son promised, and when his father's funeral took place a few days later, just before the coffin lid was screwed down he wrote out a large cheque and put it in beside his father's body.

Lord Dean of Beswick

It is rumoured that menu changes are imminent in the Members' Dining-Room in the House of Commons – Cabinet Pudding changed for Banana Slip.

Greg Knight, MP

An MP was celebrating his 25th wedding anniversary and he gave a big party for all of his friends. However, for most of the festivities he was nowhere to be seen. Eventually a friend found him near the bar, drinking heavily and looking very morose.

'Good grief', the friend said, 'why are you looking so sad? You should be celebrating with your guests.'

The MP explained: 'On our wedding night we had a violent row, and I almost killed my wife. However, the thought that I might get twenty-five years in prison made me change my mind.'

The MP continued: 'Just think', he said to his friend, 'tonight I would have been a free man.'

Michael Stern, MP

When I was the Candidate for Derby South, I was very conscious of the fact that, not only were there two principal industries in the constituency, Rolls-Royce, manufacturing highly sophisticated civil aero-engines, and British Rail, whose engineering workshops were then engaged in developing the Advanced Passenger Train, but that these two huge organisations indulged in a certain amount of rivalry at all levels.

One of the problems with jet engines is that the turbo-fan blades can be severely damaged by hitting a bird in flight. Rolls-Royce had therefore developed a gun which was used to fire birds at the fan blades at various angles and speeds in order to test the results. Since the APT was to travel at much higher speeds than any train had travelled before in this country, British Rail thought it would be a good idea to test the effect on the train of hitting a bird at maximum speed. They therefore asked Rolls-Royce if they could borrow a gun.

The gun duly arrived with a complete set of operating instructions, and was set up: the only instruction missing was how to obtain the bird to be used for the experiment. On telephoning Rolls-Royce, the BR engineer was told that Rolls-Royce had a regular order for chickens from the local butcher, and so the bird was acquired.

The results were spectacular. Hurtling from the gun, the bird smashed into the train and went straight through the front of the engine, through the complex machinery inside, out through the back of the engine and in through the front plate of the tender, where it finally came to rest. Horrified at the vast damage they had done to one of their few prototypes, British Rail again telephoned Rolls-Royce – 'What did we do wrong?' they asked. A few moments thought from the other end of the 'phone, and then 'I trust that you did defrost the bird first!'